My name is

I am **Confident** in myself!

I am **STRONG!** I am **SMART!**

I can do **ANYTHING!**

Copyright © 2021 by Aniyah Davis - Alix
All rights reserved. This book or any portion thereof
may not be reproduced or used in any
manner whatsoever without the express written
permission of the publisher except for the
use of brief quotations in a book review.
Printed in the United States of America

First Printing, 2021

This book is inspired by my boys! May you always have the confidence to chase your wildest dreams.

Love, Mom

There once was a very brave boy named Kevin. Kevin was **Smart**, **Courageous** and very very **Strong**. Kevin could do **ANYTHING!**

But Kevin wasn't always such a brave boy. He used to be **shy** and **afraid** of trying new things.

How did he become so brave, you ask? Well, Kevin's dad taught him to be **CONFIDENT!**

Whenever Kevin felt nervous or afraid, his father would tell him, "Be confident in everything you do.

You are **Smart!** You are **Strong!** You can **do Anything!**

And he did!

When Kevin was **five years** old,
he started Kindergarten. His favorite part of school was recess!

During recess, Kevin **loved** to run races and play fun games with his friends. Kevin believed he was the fastest kid
in his class.

One day, he was **challenged** by an older kid on the playground.

"Race me, Kevin! You are too **slow!** I can beat you running backwards!" laughed the kid from across the playground

Kevin began to get nervous.
"What if he beats me? What if I lose?"
Kevin thought to himself.

Before the nerves could take over, a voice **popped** in his head. It was the voice of his father! "**Don't** listen to him! Be **confident!** You are **smart**; you are **Strong!** You can do **ANYTHING!**"

And he did!

When Kevin was in middle school, he dreamed of making the **basketball team**. He and his dad **practiced** everyday after school! When it was time for tryouts, he was more than ready!

While running basketball drills in the gym, Kevin heard from behind him, "You think you can make the team? You are way **too short** to be on this team!"

Before Kevin could respond, his father's voice rang in his head, "Don't let him get to you. Remain Confident! You are **Smart**; you are **Strong**, You can do **Anything!**"

Kevin turned around and smiled at the other player." **"Watch me!** I'll make the team!"

And he did!

As Kevin grew older, the more confident he became! He had his heart set on being a **Dinosaur Expert**. Kevin could name almost every dinosaur known to man!

Becoming a **Paleontologist** was his dream and Kevin knew he would have to work hard and remain confident on his journey to **success**.

Kevin did not let anything stop him in pursuing his dreams. When things got tough, sure enough, Kevin **remembered** his father's words.

"Keep it up, son! You are **smart**, you are **strong**, you can do **anything!**"

And he did!

In fact, Kevin went on to graduate college at the top of his class and became a world-famous Paleontologist.

He even **won** the Nobel Prize for discovering a rare and unknown species of Dinosaur! When asked how he became such an outstanding man, Kevin would respond, "**I owe it to my dad!**" Kevin's father taught him that as long as he remains confident, he can achieve anything he sets his mind to.

And so can **YOU!**
As long as you remember to be **Confident!** You are **Smart**, You are **Strong**,
You can do **Anything!**

Story Vocabulary

I am BRAVE: ready to face something unknown.

I am COURAGEOUS: using your bravery to try something new.

I am CONFIDENT: sure of your abilities.

I have FAITH: to trust that everything will work out.

ABOUT THE AUTHOR

Aniyah Davis-Alix is a god fearing, dedicated wife and mother. As a graduate with a bachelors degree in Culinary Management, cooking has always been her passion. However, with a life long infatuation with creative writing and deep love for children (especially her own) she decided to premier her writing career with a children's book.

I am **Confident** in myself!
I am **STRONG!** I am **SMART!**
I can do **ANYTHING!**

Made in the USA
Middletown, DE
16 March 2022